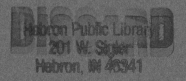

SPORTS PALACES

Thomas S. Owens

BASEBALL
PARKS

The Millbrook Press   **Brookfield, Connecticut**

To Diana Star Helmer, still

Designed by Thomas Morlock   Cover photograph of Coors Field courtesy of Corbis

Photographs courtesy of Corbis: pp. 1, 21 (© Todd Gipstein), 37 (© Lake County Museum), 40 (© Reuters NewMedia Inc.), 54 (© Reuters NewMedia Inc.), 60 (© Reuters NewMedia Inc.); Bettmann/Corbis: pp. 5, 61; National Baseball Hall of Fame Library, Cooperstown, N.Y.: pp. 7, 15 (left); AP/Wide World Photos: pp. 11, 28, 34, 43, 45; The Sporting News: pp. 15 (right), 24, 31, 33; Allsport: pp. 17 (© Matthew Stockman), 55 (© Chris Covatta), 56 (© Harry How); SportsChrome USA: pp. 47 (© Rob Tringali, Jr.), 50 (© Scott Troyanos); Archive Photos: p. 59 (© Reuters/Robert Rogers)

Library of Congress Cataloging-in-Publication Data

Owens, Tom, 1960-
Baseball parks / Thomas S. Owens.
p. cm. – (Sports palaces)
Includes bibliographical references and index.
ISBN 0-7613-1765-1 (lib. bdg.)
1. Baseball fields–United States–Juvenile literature. [1. Baseball fields.] I. Title. II.
Series.

GV879.5 .O94 2001
796.357'06'873–dc21

00–054813

Published by The Millbrook Press, Inc.

2 Old New Milford Road

Brookfield, CT 06804

www.millbrookpress.com

Printed in Hong Kong

1 3 5 4 2

Contents

1

VOICES FROM THE STANDS

A ballpark is like a home. Both are places where special things happen, a setting for memories.

Many fans can remember their first ball game and the ballpark where they saw it played. Often the sights, the sounds, the action, the crowds, even the smells are installed forever in their memories. And those who go season after season take in more. They know exactly where the best seats are, where foul balls land in the stands, where to wait to get an autograph after the game, and, of course, where to find the best snacks. The sights, the landscape, and even the lives of the locals—all are important at the perfect ballpark.

The Braves' Beautiful Palace

Baseball fan Bob Buege remembered County Stadium not as the Milwaukee Brewers home, but as the palace housing the Milwaukee Braves (who now play in Atlanta).

County Stadium was baseball's first ballpark built with taxpayer money. Building began in 1950 at a cost of $5 million. When the fan-poor Boston Braves kept losing ticket sales to the nearby Red Sox, they decided to move to a locale easier to reach by car. Milwaukee had a new, modern stadium waiting. Fans were used to baseball and to the Braves. The Braves' top minor league team played in Milwaukee through 1952.

"My first game at County Stadium was a Sunday doubleheader with the St. Louis Cardinals in July 1953," Buege said. "I was seven years old, attending with my dad. We sat in the left center field bleachers." The father and son would be two of the league record 1,826,397 fans at the stadium's first season.

"I was impressed by how green the grass looked. The stadium was packed, and fans cheered everything—player introductions, foul balls, base hits, and especially a long home run by Eddie Mathews," Buege said. "Nearly all the men in attendance wore suits and fedora-style hats. The smell of cigars permeated the air."

The young fan experienced baseball in a new way. "I don't remember the scoreboard that day, but the public address announcements of the players fascinated me—it sounded like the voice of God introducing Rip Repulski, Warren Spahn, Joe Adcock, Peanuts Lowrey. . . ballplayers' names still intrigue me."

Buege admits that, at the time, "My knowledge of baseball was rudimentary." But his dad would point and say, "Watch this guy, that's Stan Musial. He's one of the greatest hitters in the game."

Buege said, "Musial was the Cardinal fielder closest to me that day, playing left, and he looked ordinary to me."

AS THE BRAVES HOSTED THE 1957 WORLD SERIES, THEIR WELL-DRESSED FANS DISCOVERED THAT VIEWS WERE GOOD EVEN UNDER THE DOUBLE-DECKER GRANDSTANDS, BUT OUTFIELD SEATS COULD BE BACKLESS BENCHES.

WHAT FAN DOESN'T LOVE THE

GRASSY FIELD AT A BALLPARK?

THOSE STRIPES IN THE GRASS,

PATTERNS CUT INTO THE SOD, ARE

WORKS OF ART. AFTER MOWING,

GROUNDSKEEPERS USE ROLLERS ON

SOME OF THE CUT GRASS. THAT'S

HOW THE STRIPED EFFECT IS MADE.

There were other things Dad couldn't explain. For example, why did the outfielders leave their gloves on the field at the end of each half inning? (Back then, players didn't bother putting their gloves away in the dugout.) And why was Game Two called on account of darkness after eight innings, with the Braves losing 4–1?

"It was late afternoon, the sun was shining, and the stadium had lights, if needed," Buege said. Only years later did he figure out that players—and fans—had trains to catch. Getting home was a special concern, Buege said, since "County Stadium was probably the first ballpark not built in a neighborhood. It was situated on the site of a former quarry, surrounded by vast expanses of parking, most closely bordered by industrial plants, the grounds of a veterans' hospital, and rail tracks." As a result, "When you approached the ballpark, you left the real world behind," Buege said.

"My first night game, viewed from the lower grandstand, was a sensory experience— the glow of the stadium lights as the outside darkness emerged, the beautiful whiteness of the three bases and the Braves' home uniforms, the deep brown of the watered dirt infield, and again the deep green of the grass.

"The following season, a final touch completed the landscape: the addition of 'Perini's Woods.' It was a small coniferous forest planted within the park, but beyond center field's wire fence, providing a better background for batters and a bucolic freshness for fans. To the eyes of an eight-year-old, no more beautiful place could have existed. Even forty-five years later, I still love that ballpark."

The way it used to be.

Personal Park

Burton Boxerman grew up in the 1940s in St. Louis, a city with two major league teams sharing one ballpark.

"I saw both the Cardinals and Browns play there when I was a teenager," Boxerman said. "To me, there will never be a park like Sportsman's Park. It was a baseball park, not a stadium." What's the difference? "Every seat was close to the field," Boxerman said. "There was that feeling of intimacy."

Sometimes, things were too close for comfort. "The only downside to the park were the pillars, which obscured the view of those fans who sat higher than the eighth row," Boxerman said. "If you happened to sit in the wrong seat, you might have a difficult time seeing the game."

And the intimacy lasted. "Once the game ended, fans were allowed to go down on the field, run the bases, and even sit in the dugout," Boxerman remembered. "The door in right field opened after the game and it served as an exit to Grand Avenue, where one could catch the local streetcar and depart for home. After the game, the players left their dugouts and the fans were able to greet them before the players made their way to the dressing rooms."

One Good-Smelling Stadium

Anthony Craine began attending Cubs games at Chicago's Wrigley Field (see page 24) in 1969.

"I'm hard-pressed to think of an actual bad seat at Wrigley Field. To be honest with you, I think they're all good," Craine said. "My favorite Wrigley seats, I think, are in the upper-deck box seats, right behind the plate. That's where you get the best view of the pitches and the best overview of the action."

Craine's worst Wrigley seat was one of the last seats available at a sold-out game.

"I sat in the lower deck in the last section out toward right field, in the last row—right above the vent from one of the grills downstairs. I smelled like a hamburger by the time I left! In those seats, you're so far back underneath the upper deck—and the luxury boxes—that you see almost none of the sky. I had to lean forward in order to see the clock at the top of the scoreboard," Craine added.

But even this seat had its good points. "It protected me from the rain—and it did rain that day!" Craine admitted. "I've practically lived at Wrigley Field." And, like a lot of other Chicago kids, he didn't leave baseball at the park.

"In the 1960s, a good number of the Cubs players lived in the northwest suburbs, which meant that they had to take the Kennedy Expressway home, along with a fair number of fans returning home from the game," Craine said. "To avoid the traffic—and to avoid being recognized in bumper-to-bumper traffic—the players would take sort of a shortcut.

"They would take a side street all the way to the expressway entrance," Craine continued. "My sister-in-law grew up in the neighborhood there, and she and her siblings and friends would wait after games for players to drive by. They'd do anything they could to get [players] to stop and sign a few autographs—and often they succeeded."

A Friend of Fenway

Baseball author Bill Nowlin began taking his son to games at Boston's Fenway Park when the boy was only six weeks old!

To most Red Sox fans, there's no ballpark like Fenway (see page 21). But like any ballpark, Fenway has its peculiarities, too.

"There are some very strange seats out in the boxes in Sections 1 and 2," Nowlin remembered. "The seats are at angles to each other in such a way that people's knees touch each other at about a 60-degree angle."

But different can be good. "Two of my favorite seats," Nowlin said, "though not the 'best,' are the last seat in Section 33 and the first seat in Section 28. Both are single row seats—the 'row' consists of one seat only!" No one can complain about the loud guy in the next seat hogging the armrests.

An Astros Voice Speaks

Bill Brown became the Houston Astros announcer in 1987, working in the Astrodome (see page 17) until the building's last season in 1999.

"The Astrodome differed in several ways from other ballparks," Brown recalled. "It was known for many years as a tough hitters' park, but in [later] years the hitters had more success there. A 'dead air' park like that can be very friendly to flyball pitchers." In other words, there was never a wind blowing in Houston's domed park like there was in hitter-helping, gusty Wrigley Field.

But perhaps the Astrodome's biggest difference was that "the fans sat in cushioned, theater-type seats. The comfort of the environment seemed to take away from the feeling of being in a baseball stadium," Brown said. Because the park had "a more laid-back atmosphere . . . the fans really didn't respond until something big happened."

While a team can abandon a ballpark, fans who witness games there can keep the place alive forever—at least, in their memories.

SOMETIMES, STADIUMS HAVE MANY LIVES. WHEN THE COLT .45S' STADIUM IN HOUSTON WAS TORN DOWN TO MAKE PARKING LOT SPACE FOR THE NEW ASTRODOME IN 1965, THE OLD BALLPARK WAS SHIPPED TO MEXICO AND REBUILT THERE— PIECE BY PIECE!

2

BEST SEATS IN THE BALLPARK?

Fans may think they know ballparks. They may have sat in the best and worst seats.

But players have a whole different view of ballparks. All year long, they play there, which also means they work there. Sometimes, it seems they live there. Former players, removed from the daily pressure of winning and losing, get better views of what their places of employment were...and were not.

Changing Times

Infielder Jerry Coleman played in six World Series with the New York Yankees during his short career, from 1949 through 1957. Upon retirement, he became a baseball broadcaster on TV and radio for more than thirty years, taking time out to manage the San Diego Padres in 1980. Few men have had such exposure to so many ballparks, past and present.

Coleman pointed out that the parks built before 1950 weren't designed just for a small, cozy baseball experience. A designer's main concern was to fit the park into a preexisting cityscape.

"In the old days, ballparks were built depending on street dimensions," Coleman said. "They couldn't move the streets surrounding the parks." And there was no room for huge parking lots to surround the sites like moats around a castle.

But for older sites like Yankee Stadium, "nobody seemed to have cars, anyway," Coleman said. Playing

Yankee Stadium's stately blue and white walls rise up from its Bronx neighborhood. The 1974-75 remodeling removed all sight barriers for all seats.

in the Bronx, deep in the city, meant that players and their families might not live nearby. "We [newer Yankees] stayed in Manhattan by taking the subway out. The D train took fifteen to twenty minutes. It would zip you right there."

Public transportation plays an important part in baseball history. The Brooklyn Dodgers owed their name to public transport. The team was named after trolley dodgers (people who'd duck oncoming streetcars).

But times have changed, Coleman noted. "The Ballpark in [Arlington] Texas? It's out in the middle of a field somewhere. You'd have to drive!"

A Never-Ending Outfield?

New York Giants catcher Harry "The Horse" Danning recalled the benefits and drawbacks of his home ballpark, the Polo Grounds (see page 37), during his career of 1933–1942.

Danning the catcher and his pitchers appreciated the huge distances to the outfield that prevented home runs (as far as 505 feet—154 meters—to the center field fence). Danning the hitter saw the field design differently.

"The outfielders gave you the lines, and bunched you in the middle," he said. "It was almost impossible to hit a ball between the outfielders."

With shorter distances to the left and right field walls, outfielders could keep more hits in front of them, yielding fewer bases.

Despite being a typical slow-running catcher, Danning benefited once from the Eddie Grant Memorial in center field. The 5-foot-high (1.5-meter) high stone marker was placed at the base of the outfield wall in 1921, to honor the only active player (then a Giant) killed in World War I. Oddly, the ground rules of the ballpark said that the monument was in play. Danning smacked a drive that bounced behind the marker. In the confusion that followed, he lumbered around the bases for an inside-the-park home run.

The Pride of Pittsburgh

Lenny Yochim pitched for the 1951 and 1954 Pittsburgh Pirates. Their park, Forbes Field, stood in the shadow of the Cathedral of Learning, one of the tallest buildings on the University of Pittsburgh campus. "Going from the Class A South Atlantic [minor]

League at age 22, you can believe [Forbes] was a beautiful park," he remembered. "Forbes Field, like most parks of its time, had an aura about it, a wonderful smell. The clubhouse had its gripping aroma! The neighborhood was a mixture of residences and business. People around the area were always busy."

With time away from the game, almost any ballplayer can remember more than scores. He can recall the distance to the outfield fences, how hard or easily homers came, the sun and shadow while hitting or fielding, the way the grounds were kept up.

Gail Harris, whose six-year career was highlighted by twenty homers for the 1958 Tigers, summed up the thrill of players being front and center in their era's top ballparks. "I didn't accomplish a lot," he said, "but I did have a great seat to watch them play!"

WHEN VETERANS STADIUM OPENED IN PHILADELPHIA IN 1971, THE FIRST PITCH WASN'T THROWN. IT WAS DROPPED—BY HELICOPTER! PHILLIES CATCHER MIKE RYAN CAUGHT THE CEREMONIAL SINKER.

3

THE BIRTH OF BALLPARKS

Fans love to call stadiums "ballparks." After all, the whole idea of a park is fun and inviting.

The first ballparks were simple: some small wooden bleachers and a fence. This allowed for the first tickets to be sold. Most seats were near the infield. Other fans would stand along the baselines, or even in the outfield.

Once baseball's appeal grew, teams knew they could sell thousands of tickets to every game. The challenge was where to put the fans. The answer: bigger stadiums. Boston built baseball's first double-decked grandstand with the rebuilt South End Grounds in 1888. The capacity for the Beaneaters (later the Braves) was 6,800 seats.

Yet, while teams were creating stadiums in record time to respond to fan demand, stadiums disappeared with the same speed. The all-wood structures burned easily. Teams took the blazes in stride, though, usually building a look-alike facility on the same grounds.

Consider League Park in Cleveland, Ohio. An 1892 game was postponed when a lightning bolt struck the park and set it ablaze. Columns were hastily raised to steady the double-decked grandstands, and the game was ready to go on—until fans discovered that the columns blocked their view.

Philadelphia's Shibe Park was the first baseball stadium constructed primarily of concrete and steel.

It opened in 1909, as did Pittsburgh's Forbes Field. Shibe could seat 20,000 in its opening season. Forbes could host 23,000 ticket holders. Eight more teams quickly created "modern" parks of such burn-resistant materials.

Ever Changing

By the 1950s, teams demanded better locations for stadiums. Instead of appealing to only one city's fans, the right stadium could reach out to ticket buyers from several states.

PHILADELPHIA'S SHIBE PARK WAS THE FIRST TO FEATURE FOLDING-CHAIR SEATS. MOST OF THE STADIUM WAS ENCLOSED AND ROOFED.

The poorly attended Boston Braves were moved to Milwaukee, Wisconsin, after the 1952 season. The new location would be automobile-friendly. Tons of parking and easy access from major highways meant that fans from surrounding states would come. In past decades, a team might rely on selling tickets within its own city.

A second phase of ballpark building commenced in the 1960s. Major League Baseball had created a new guideline for playing field dimensions:

> Rule 1.04(a): Any Playing Field constructed by a professional club after June 1, 1958, shall provide a minimum distance of 325 feet [99 meters] from home base to the nearest fence, stand or other obstruction on the right and left field foul lines, and a minimum distance of 400 feet [122 meters] to the center field fence.

As always, the baselines still stretched 90 feet (27.5 meters), and the pitching mound was $60\frac{1}{2}$ feet (18.44 meters) from home plate. But foul territory wasn't included in the rule. Teams could decide how many top-priced seats to squeeze near the field.

A fear of home run explosions may have caused the ruling. The Dodgers had recently moved to Los Angeles, California, and were playing in the converted Memorial Coliseum. Made for football or Olympic events, the stadium was an odd fit for baseball. The left field screen was just 250 feet (76 meters) from home plate. Despite a 42-foot-high (13-meter) screen, the makeshift ballpark was turning windblown pop-ups into homers. The Dodgers remained in the homer haven only through 1961. Then, in 1962, the team moved to a new stadium—

still in Los Angeles, on the site where orange groves once stood. The stadium, nestled in a hillside notch called Chavez Ravine, gave fans a palm tree-dotted view overlooking the city.

When touring ballparks in Japan in 1956, Dodger owner Walter O'Malley "discovered" dugout-level seats, which gave fans the feeling of sitting right on the field. O'Malley had a background in architecture, and was able to turn ideas he liked into reality for his own park. It wasn't long before the Dodgers had dugout-level seats, too.

The Dodgers remained one of the National League's most competitive teams in the 1960s. Their stadium remained in the news, too. Inspired by nearby Disneyland and Hollywood studios, the Dodgers briefly offered stagecoaches as "fan movers" to the stadium and its parking lot—an experiment that got a lot of press. Some ideas never got a chance. Dodger Stadium once contemplated a sort of "drive in" baseball. Terraced parking would have allowed fans to park closer than ever to their seats. Safety inspectors disallowed the design, fearing accidents.

The Revolutionary '60s

In 1965, Houston shocked the baseball world with the Astrodome. Who ever heard of playing baseball indoors? Those who thought it strange had probably never been to a game in Houston's old Colt .45 stadium. At that stadium ushers used to march through the cramped, humid aisles spraying mosquito repellent.

Ushers in the new Astrodome dressed in astronaut costumes during the park's first season, stressing Houston's connection to NASA. Air conditioning lured fans to the world's first domed stadium, where a huge animated scoreboard stretched 474 feet (144 meters).

But the Astrodome wasn't perfect. With a lack of sunshine, grass fields died. Replanting didn't help. At first, the dead grass was spray-painted green. Then, in 1966, artificial turf was installed, and named "Astroturf" in honor of the ballpark.

Also in 1966, St. Louis sparked interest in multipurpose stadiums with the opening of the circular

HOUSTON'S ASTRODOME WAS THE FIRST INDOOR BALLPARK, THE FIRST WITH CLIMATE CONTROL, AND THE FIRST TO USE ASTROTURF. FANS AT THIS 1996 GAME BETWEEN THE ASTROS AND CUBS BENEFIT FROM THE UNIQUE SCOREBOARD CIRCLING THE OUTFIELD.

Busch Stadium. Although football games had been played in ballparks since the 1920s, this field (which also boasted artificial turf) was designed to be easily reconfigured for nonbaseball events.

In the past, many baseball stadiums converted to football would still show dirt basepaths and a bare pitcher's mound under the gridiron stripes. Now, with Astroturf, the ground could be covered with a layer containing football markings. Or, the turf could be remarked easily. In some ballparks, fans may have compared this to rolling up the rug.

Also in the 1960s, ballparks such as the Astrodome or Dodger Stadium began trying to attract the richest fans. These teams offered loges, or private spaces from which big spenders could see games. In later years, loges were called luxury suites or boxes. They often look like small apartments built into the stands.

The Memorable '70s

The 1970s was a notable decade in stadium history. Following Busch Stadium's design, look-alike circular stadiums became the fashion for many major league cities. Cities hoped more events in these locations would bring more income throughout the year. But some fans described the ring-shaped stadiums as ashtrays or toilet bowls.

Montreal scored the National League's first retractable roof in 1977 when the Expos moved into Olympic Stadium, a multipurpose facility created for the Olympic Games a year earlier. Actually, the Expos had only the promise of a retracting roof until 1988, a decade-long delay caused by too many mechanical problems and too little money. In 1989, the worries ended when the roof was converted to a permanently closed position.

But baseball's 1970s gem was Royals Stadium, opened in Kansas City in 1973. For fan comfort, every seat is angled toward second base. Some 322 feet (98 meters) of waterfalls and fountains stretch beyond the center field fence, able to squirt and react to fan cheers or Royals successes.

Back to Basics

The 1992 opening of Oriole Park at Baltimore's Camden Yards restored the idea of creating ballparks as baseball-only facilities in urban surroundings. The HOK Sports Facility Group conceived Baltimore's wonder, giving it an arched brick facade to blend in with the existing neighborhood. These same architects were responsible for seven of the eleven ballparks opened through 2000.

Designers gave teams—and fans—what each wanted. Teams wanted more concessions. Fans wanted more restrooms and wider aisles. Yet fans also wanted ballparks to look and feel like smaller landmarks of the past. So architects reduced the number of seats. Did the loss of seats bother team owners concerned about the bottom line? Not at all. They simply raised the ticket prices.

BEYOND THE RIGHT FIELD BLEACHERS OF ORIOLES PARK AT CAMDEN YARDS IS EUTAW STREET. THE TEAM PLACES A BASEBALL-SIZED MARKER IN THE CONCRETE THERE FOR EACH SLUGGER WHO HOMERS OUT OF THE BALLPARK.

4

A FABLED FOURSOME

As the 1999 season began, only four stadiums had surpassed their seventy-fifth birthdays—Wrigley Field in Chicago, Fenway Park in Boston, Tiger Stadium in Detroit, and Yankee Stadium in New York City.

The four ballparks were twice as old as any other active stadium in the American or National League. They reminded some fans of another park: Jurassic.

How long could these aging parks survive? Their ages made them seem like dinosaurs. All faced extinction. Two ballparks tied for "oldest" honors: Fenway Park and Tiger Stadium. Both had opened on April 20, 1912.

Always Fenway

The Boston ballpark has kept the same name through the years—though, sometimes, in the 1910s and '20s, it was called Fenway Park Grounds. Never seating more than 35,000, the ballpark remained the American League's smallest for decades. The reddish-brick exterior and the sea of blueish green covering the insides of the irregularly shaped ballpark have always been there, reminding a few visitors of watermelons.

But Fenway's most famous landmark evolved over the years. "The Green Monster" is the name for Fenway's famous 37-foot-tall (11-meter) wall in left

FENWAY'S "GREEN MONSTER" ONCE WASN'T GREEN; ADVERTISEMENTS
COVERED THE BARRIER BEFORE 1947. FENWAY'S BEST SEATS MAY BE
INSIDE THE SCOREBOARD, WHERE WORKERS UPDATE RESULTS MANUALLY.

field. However, it wasn't painted solid green until 1947. Before that, assorted advertisements and billboards plastered the wall.

Left fielders still worry about which way hits may bounce off that wall. But it was even worse before the Monster was coated in hard plastic in 1976. Till then, the wall was a wooden framework covered in tin. A hit against a wood beam created a dead thud. A ball caroming off tin offered lively, wild bounces.

Atop the Green Monster, Fenway visitors can see a clue to the ballpark's urban history of being squeezed into the heart of a city. The 23-foot (7-meter) screen topping the wall was added for the good of Boston. Or, precisely, to benefit Landsdowne Street. Without the screen for partial protection, the shopkeepers and citizens on the surrounding block faced a hailstorm of baseballs every game.

The Red Sox created a political drama beginning in 1999. They unveiled plans for a new stadium to be built within sight of old Fenway by the 2003 season. No plans for modernizing Fenway were included as an alternative by the team. The Red Sox abandoned hopes of acquiring land and opening a new facility by their target date, however, as city officials worried over public spending. Team threats of moving to a city more likely to provide land and tax dollars for a new ballpark began appearing in Boston media the next year. Would baseball's other three surviving elderly parks fare better?

Made in Michigan

The site of Detroit's Tiger Stadium had been used for major league baseball since 1901. First came Bennett Park, which was built on the space in 1896, with its home plate situated in what later became Tiger Stadium's right field. Before Bennett, the grounds were a hay market.

Detroit's ballpark has been called a lot of names over the years: from 1912 to 1937, it was called Navin Field after then-boss Frank Navin. From 1938 to 1960, new owner Walter Briggs could choose the name. He chose Briggs Stadium. After that, the park took its team's name.

The fortresslike landmark at the corner of Michigan and Trumbull was full of oddities. Outside the entrance to one clubhouse was a sign: VISITORS' CLUBHOUSE—NO VISITORS ALLOWED.

Starting in 1912, a 125-foot (38-meter) flagpole stood at the base of the center field wall—in fair territory.

Not all parts of the Tigers' park were so amusing. Nearly 5,000 seats were behind a foul pole or pillar, or had some partially blocked view.

The ballpark grew to a capacity of nearly 53,000 seats in 1938. Cherry Street, the northern border of Tiger Stadium, was closed. This allowed the team to build a larger, double-decked grandstand in left and center field that made the park enclosed.

But Tiger Stadium's cheap seats in right field were the ones fans loved best. They were like no other right field perches in baseball; the "porch" extended closer to the right field than the lower deck by 10 feet (3 meters).

The Detroit ballpark defied trendy changes in baseball. It was the last American League stadium to install lights for night games in 1948.

As Tiger Stadium advanced in age, Tiger players tried to remain good-humored about their aging field. Many Detroit players joked that you could tell members of the Tigers from other players by checking their heads for bumps. Bumps? Tiger Stadium was infamous for having the lowest dugout roofs in baseball.

Fans feared for Tiger Stadium's survival in the early 1970s. As the city planned the Silverdome in nearby Pontiac as a home for football's Lions, fans wondered if this would become another multipurpose facility, housing Detroit's baseball team, too. John Fetzer, then owner of the Tigers, ended the worry by saying he didn't really own the team. "This franchise belongs to the inner city of Detroit," Fetzer said. "I'm just the caretaker."

Nevertheless, fans of the historic stadium didn't stop their rallies. The Tiger Stadium Fan Club was born. Ballpark historian Phil Lowry succeeded in getting Tiger Stadium honored by the U.S. Department of the Interior with a spot on the National Register of Historic Sites. The Fan Club organized "group hugs" in 1988 and 1990—where a group would gather to hug Tiger Stadium!

When the team signed a lease to play in Tiger Stadium through 2008, Tiger fans began to breathe easy. But this sense of security was short-lived. In 1997, team officials broke ground for a new stadium. They said the lack of parking near Tiger Stadium was a major issue. And the parking problem was made worse by the fact that the nearby neighborhoods did not seem safe to some fans. The city and team agreed to end their contract.

By the start of the 2000 season, the Tigers moved to the new Comerica Park (see page 43). Their former habitat of Tiger Stadium, it was rumored, would be torn down to make way for low-income housing.

Life Before the Cubs

Before becoming a major league venue, Wrigley Field hosted games by the player-organized Federal League, a better-paying alternative to the major leagues. But the league survived just two years, 1914–1915. Wrigley is its only surviving site.

In 1916, the Cubs moved into Wrigley. At their first home game, a live bear named Joa attended as

THE FARTHEST UPPER DECK SEATS AT WRIGLEY FIELD STILL OFFER A VIEW OF THE BRICK, IVY-COVERED WALLS, HIGHLIGHTED BY BLUE AND WHITE TRIM. FANS CAN SEE LAKE MICHIGAN IN THE DISTANCE.

the team mascot. During that July, Joa lived in a cage outside the ballpark.

Over the years the ballpark underwent improvements. In 1937, Wrigley's unique hand-operated scoreboard was built by Bill Veeck, who'd later become a famed owner of other teams. The scoreboard measures 27 by 75 feet (8 by 23 meters). Signs with numbers are slid into holes to note inning-by-inning scores around the leagues. The same year, Veeck planted 200 Boston ivy and 350 Japanese bittersweet plants to cover the red brick outfield walls.

Those vine-covered walls have produced some unforgettable plays. Balls that are hit into the ivy and stick there are limited to a ground-rule double—but the outfielder has to alert the umpire to the problem! Pirates outfielder Roberto Clemente, trying to stop a Cubs runner, reached into the vines, grabbed, and threw. But what he threw was an empty drink cup, litter from a bleacher fan, not the baseball.

Another of Veeck's landscaping ideas didn't live. He tried adding eight Chinese elm trees to highlight the wooden bleacher stairs. But winds from nearby Lake Michigan blew the leaves off. Nevertheless, Wrigley Field's appearance was so much a part of the game experience that, during the 1930s, groundskeeper Bobby Dorr lived in a six-room apartment within the ballpark, near the left field corner. Few knew of Dorr's residency then, and few may know today whose idea it was to have an "in-house" groundskeeper. In fact, if other teams knew of Dorr's on-call success, every ballpark may have housed a groundskeeper.

Wrigley Field is also famous for what did not happen there during the 1940s. Team owner P. K. Wrigley had purchased lights to be installed for night games, a new idea and an immense expense at the time. However, on December 8, 1941, one day after the Japanese bombed American ships in Pearl Harbor, the Cubs owner donated the lights to aid the U.S. military's defense. As a result, the Cubs would not play their first night game until 1988.

Unknown to many Cubs fans, the 1988 game was the second night game hosted at Wrigley. In July 1943, two all-star teams made up of members of the All American Girls Professional Baseball League played a fundraiser for the Red Cross, using temporary lights set up on the field.

Wrigley Field has always been known for its traditions. A fan favorite is the raising of the postgame pennant. After each game, one of two pennants appears atop the flagpole: one with a W (for win) or one with an L (for loss). The Cubs still display their win or loss to everyone, not just ticket buyers. Some fans laugh that the *L* is a white flag, the famed signal for surrender.

Home of the Bronx Bombers

New York's Yankee Stadium, built in 1923, is a senior citizen of baseball. But to some, Yankee Stadium seems much newer.

The stadium closed from 1974 to 1975 for remodeling. During that time, the Yankees moved to Flushing, New York, to share Shea Stadium with the Mets. When the Yanks returned to their own stadium in 1976, they found a number of changes.

The monuments in center field were fenced off, no longer considered in play. These three monuments honor former players including homer king Babe Ruth. (The stadium's nickname is "The House That Ruth Built.") Some fans mistake the tombstone-like tributes as outfield gravesites of famed Yankees!

Another change was the removal of the famed copper border that ran along the entire roof, looking like an upside-down picket fence. The decorative facade once scalloped the entire grandstand roof like icing on a layer cake. Now only a section of the old copper border frames the bleachers in center field.

When Yankee Stadium approached its seventy-fifth birthday in 1998, the team and fans alike faced a shock. A 500-pound (227-kilogram) piece of steel fell from a ceiling, crushing several seats. Luckily, the accident happened during an off-day, when the stadium was empty, but the incident showed that Yankee Stadium was aging and once again in need of repair.

The Yankees played their next game at Shea Stadium, waiting for a safety inspection of the required repairs.

Some reports blamed the city for not inspecting the ballpark structures regularly. Other accounts claimed the Yankees didn't want to spend money for stadium upkeep, in hope that the city would help build the team a new ballpark faster. Team owner George Steinbrenner had dropped hints for years that he'd welcome a new stadium, but seemed to fear that the public would say he was trying to destroy baseball history.

As a new century began, old ballparks were in jeopardy. Tiger Stadium was extinct. The trio of other parks remained endangered species, three bits of living history with worrisome life spans.

5

BYGONE BALLPARKS

When a person dies, his or her obituary is printed in the newspaper. When was he born? Where did he live? How and when did he die? And, most importantly, what was his life like—what did he accomplish?

Obituaries, of a sort, have also been printed after the "deaths" of famed ballparks. And, just as when any loved one dies, written remembrances of ballparks tell about more than appearances, more than just the architecture or building materials.

Tiger Stadium got its fair share of loving obituaries. Other gone-but-not-forgotten ballparks include five on the East Coast and four in the Midwest.

Ebbets Field, Brooklyn, New York
(1913–1957)

Sitting on just $4\frac{1}{2}$ acres (1.8 hectares), the Dodgers' old red-brick home in Brooklyn, New York, was decorated like a home—for baseball players. A marble floor patterned like stitches on a baseball greeted fans who entered through the main entrance rotunda. A chandelier shaped like a fan of baseball bats shone overhead.

Even the gaudy billboards in the outfield seemed like a part of the game. The *h* or *e* in the Schaefer Beer ad would light up to signal if the

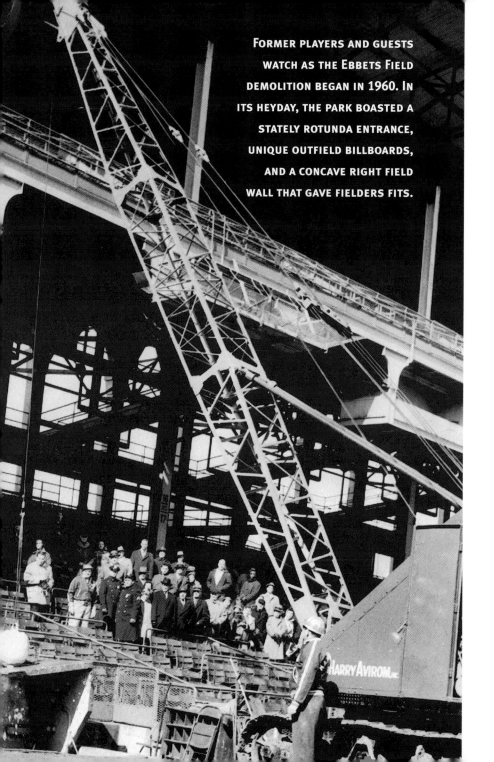

batter would be credited with a hit or an error. "Hit Sign, Win Suit" said a sign advertising men's clothing retailer Abe Stark. His target tempted batters, although it was only 3 by 30 feet (1 by 9 meters) at the base of the right field wall beneath the scoreboard.

By 1956, Dodgers team owner Walter O'Malley had started worrying out loud about the problems of the aging Ebbets Field. Neighborhood crime and a lack of parking were among his complaints. A ballpark which seated only 32,000 and offered limited ticket sales may have been a greater worry. In a move which hinted that the Dodgers might not be Brooklynites forever, O'Malley arranged for the team to play more than a dozen regular-season games at a minor league stadium in Jersey City, New Jersey.

After the 1956 season, O'Malley sold Ebbets Field to a housing developer. The deal said the Dodgers could play up to five more years in the ballpark—if a new local facility was planned. But New York's leaders argued about locations and costs, and the team ownership lost patience. Finally, on October 9, 1957, O'Malley announced that the Dodgers would move immediately to Los Angeles, California.

The old ballpark was torn down in 1960. As if going to a funeral, nearly two hundred people, including current and former Dodgers, watched as a wrecking ball painted like a baseball began crushing the remains of Ebbets Field. The demolition company later sold gold-plated stadium bricks for a dollar apiece. Flowerpots filled with infield dirt were free. An auction of Ebbets' contents brought a mere $2,300.

Polo Grounds, New York, New York
(1891–1957 Giants, 1962–1963 Mets)
Was it shaped more like a horseshoe or a bathtub?

In the beginning, the Polo Grounds in New York City was, in fact, an oval (see page 37), much like a racetrack, and the outfield was unfenced. Why? It was a drive-in ballpark; horse-drawn carriages could park in the open end and see a game!

The locker rooms weren't under the dugout, but at grandstand level in center field. A short flight of open stairs led down from each locker room and onto center field. Fans could watch their heroes descend and march across the field to their dugouts.

After the Giants departed for San Francisco following the 1957 season, the Polo Grounds seemed old and forgotten. The ballpark hosted the just-formed expansion team, the New York Mets, for its first two seasons (1962–1963), only by making $250,000 in repairs. The Polo Grounds was demolished on April 10, 1964, using the same wrecking ball that razed Ebbets Field. The land would be used for a public housing complex.

SINGER FRANK SINATRA BUILT A MUSICAL MONUMENT TO ONE BALLPARK. IN 1973, HE RECORDED "THERE USED TO BE A BALLPARK HERE," A SONG INSPIRED BY THE DESTRUCTION OF BROOKLYN'S EBBETS FIELD. WORDS AND MUSIC WERE BY JOE RAPOSO, WHO ALSO WROTE THE *SESAME STREET* THEME.

Shibe Park, Philadelphia, Pennsylvania
(1909–1954 American League Athletics, 1938–1970 National League Phillies)

Shibe, the first park constructed of concrete and steel (see page 15), had two lives. Shibe was first home to the Philadelphia Athletics. Then, the Phillies shared the stadium. When the A's saw slipping ticket sales in the 1930s, they didn't buy more advertising—they built a bigger outfield wall. Why? Owners of buildings across the street had constructed their own rooftop bleachers outside the park and were selling cheap tickets to fans. The A's new 50-foot (15-meter) right field wall built in 1935 took care of these "Peeping Toms" and nonpaying peeping fans of other names. Three years later, the Phillies became park tenants, sharing the privacy fence.

The ballpark was renamed Connie Mack Stadium in 1952, honoring the man who managed and owned the Athletics for fifty years. When Mack wasn't seen during games leading the team from the dugout (though never wearing a uniform like other managers!), he'd work in an office behind home plate. Fans could only see the office from outside the stadium's main entrance, where a small, gold dome topped Mack's space with the dignity of a church or state capitol.

Although the A's moved to Kansas City in 1955, the Phillies stayed on until 1970, when they moved into their new Veterans Stadium. As early as 1956, Philadelphia fans might have guessed the aging Shibe Park was losing its place as a baseball palace. Yankee Stadium's used scoreboard was installed as a hand-me-down addition.

On August 20, 1971, two youths started a fire in the abandoned stadium. After two hours, the grandstand roof collapsed. In June 1976, the ballpark was demolished to make room for low-income housing.

Comiskey Park, Chicago, Illinois
(1910–1990)

Was the original site of Chicago's Comiskey Park once a junkyard? White Sox players and fans saw the truth unearthed during a 1940s contest. White Sox infielder Luke Appling stopped play during a home game, kicking at what seemed to be a rock in the dirt. The surprise object was a half-buried copper pot.

But Comiskey Park itself was anything but a dump. In 1960, owner Bill Veeck unveiled an exploding scoreboard. Fireworks and assorted sound effects roared for more than thirty seconds every time the home team got a homer.

Comiskey Park appeared like a church to some. Arched windows (later just open spaces) between the first and second decks opened baseball to the

THE ONLY PART OF ALL-BRICK COMISKEY PARK NOT COVERED BY THE GRANDSTAND ROOF WAS CENTER FIELD. THIS PHOTO SHOWS THAT WHITE SOX FANS CAME BY THE CARLOADS, EVEN IN THE 1930S.

world. To others, the ballpark was all amusement park. Two restaurants beneath the stands, enclosed with wire fencing, combined with fenced-off picnic areas under the outfield stands (including one called "The Bull Ring"), made it appear that fans were kept like caged zoo animals beside the field.

In 1991, the White Sox opened a new stadium across the street from the old, but they kept the old name. The new parking lot occupies the first ballpark's space.

Sportsman's Park, St. Louis, Missouri
(1902–1953 Browns, 1920–1966 Cardinals)
Like double-duty Shibe Park, Sportsman's Park hosted both the St. Louis Cardinals and the St. Louis Browns until the Browns became the Baltimore Orioles in 1954. Browns owner Bill Veeck sold the ballpark to Cardinals team owner Gussie Busch in 1953, a year before the "Brownies" flew to Maryland. Busch wanted to rename his purchase "Budweiser Stadium." When the League objected, the owner settled for "Busch Stadium" in 1955.

St. Louis fans may remember lots of near-miss homers at Sportsman's. From 1929 to 1955, the right field pavilion was enclosed with a tall wire screen. Before that, homers needed to travel only 310 feet

(94 meters) to clear the fence. Line drives against the screen often wound up as doubles. The screen came down in 1955.

When Busch built a new stadium for the Cardinals in 1966, he gave the land where the old stadium rested to a local boys' club.

Crosley Field, Cincinnati, Ohio
(1884-1970)
Known as Redland Field before being renamed Crosley Field for the new team owner in 1934, the Cincinnati baseball site had a long history and went through many renovations. The first ballpark, built in 1884, burned down in 1901. The second wooden structure, built in 1902, was known as the Palace of the Fans. It was modernized with a concrete-and-steel design to open the 1912 season.

Baseball history was made in Cincinnati when the sport's first night game was played on May 24, 1935. But reporters didn't cover this or other early Crosley Field games in comfort. Before 1938, there was no press box. Reporters sat in the second deck. Players didn't fare much better; teams had dressing rooms under the left field stands.

In left field, most fly balls were adventures. Starting 15 feet (4.5 meters) from the fence, the

ground in left field rose in a 4-foot (1.2-meter) incline. The tiny hill seemed like a mountain to some outfielders, who'd topple from the terrace while watching seemingly easy fly balls fall in for hits.

In January 1937, nearby Mill Creek overflowed, flooding the ballpark. Just for fun, Reds pitcher Lee Grissom and a front office employee steered a rowboat over the submerged outfield fences.

Crosley Field closed June 24, 1970. Its home plate was dug up and reinstalled at the new Cincinnati ballpark, Riverfront Stadium. In 1972, Crosley was demolished. The land has become part of an industrial zone, hosting various businesses.

Forbes Field, Pittsburgh, Pennsylvania
(1909–1970)

In most ballparks, catchers have to cover about 60 feet (18 meters) of ground from home plate to the backstop. In Forbes Field, the distance was almost twice as much—110 feet (33.5 meters). That is why some reporters called a catcher in Forbes Field the team's "fourth outfielder."

The deepest part of the park was 457 feet (139 meters) to the left center field wall. To fill up the space, the team once kept the batting practice cage there on the field. A ball hitting the cage was still considered in play—a fair ball.

In the 1920s, you could find more than baseball under the left field grandstand. Cars were sold and fixed there! By 1938, Forbes boasted a then-modern

FORBES FIELD SERVED THE PIRATES FOR SIXTY-TWO YEARS. NOW ALL THAT REMAINS OF THE ORNATE STRUCTURE IS THE OUTFIELD WALL OVERSHADOWED BY THE UNIVERSITY OF PITTSBURGH'S CATHEDRAL OF LEARNING (IN THE BACKGROUND).

first: an elevator for fans to use to reach the top level of the grandstand.

The edge of the University of Pittsburgh campus neighbored Forbes Field. Views from the ballpark didn't match many urban stadiums. One of the tallest buildings on campus, the Cathedral of Learning, loomed over the outfield wall. Groves of trees from Schenley Park added to the unforgettable, unusual background.

The University of Pittsburgh now uses the grounds where Forbes once stood. The school has preserved part of the stadium wall over which the 1960 World Series-winning homer hit by Pirate Bill Mazeroski passed.

Griffith Stadium, Washington, D.C.
(1892–1899, 1903–1961)

Griffith Stadium might have had the strangest center field in history. Jammed against the fence were five houses and backyards. When the park was built, the original homeowners refused to sell, so the park was constructed around the holdouts.

No matter how dismal the season looked for the Senators, their stadium was usually packed with fans for the home opener. The U.S. president would appear from the seats next to the first base dugout to throw out a ceremonial first pitch. Of course, government officials and other celebrities would turn up for the yearly ceremony, giving the team at least one exciting game each year.

When the Senators moved and became the Minnesota Twins to start the 1961 season, baseball expanded. The major leagues granted Washington, D.C., a replacement team. A new stadium was built for 1962 and Griffith Stadium was demolished three years later.

Today, Howard University Hospital sits in the location where the Senators played. But no marker or plaque has ever been placed to tell people that the site once hosted professional baseball.

Progress is paving over past baseball palaces. Look while you can.

6

COLLECTING MEMORIES

Devoted ballpark followers have found ways to keep more than memories. They have built collections to help remember some of their favorite baseball settings. Tom Crabtree is an example. He's collected stadium postcards for ten years, and has compiled the hobby's first comprehensive checklist and price guide for past postcards.

The Collecting Challenge

"I decided I was going to collect one postcard from each ballpark, past and present," Crabtree said of his hobby beginnings. "I still haven't fulfilled that goal, [though] I probably have over three thousand postcards of ballparks, 99 percent being major league ballparks."

The oldest image is of Exposition Park in Pittsburgh, taken in 1896. The newest is Seattle's Safeco Field, opened in mid-1999. Crabtree says his postcard views of stadiums fall into three types: about 50 percent interiors, 30 percent aerial (overhead shots), and 20 percent exteriors.

Crabtree's advice to new ballparks postcard collectors is simple. "With all the new parks coming out now, try to get what you can of each of them. For these, you can get them all now while they are cheap (twenty-five cents to a dollar each). Try to find someone in the new cities to exchange cards with. "I'm sure people there would like a pen pal, too." Crabtree says postcards are like windows to baseball's—and America's—past.

"You can learn a lot about the architecture and the culture at the same time. The old parks (like Wrigley Field) are in neighborhoods, and you can see that in the postcards," he noted. "You can see in the 1960s and '70s the multipurpose stadiums that all look alike. Place a postcard of each of the interiors of these cookie-cutter stadiums on your table and try to pick out which is Cincinnati, which is Pittsburgh, and which is Philadelphia. Hard to do! Now look at the interiors of the new parks (Coors Field in Denver, Baltimore's Camden Yards, Ballpark at Arlington, etc.). How similar are they?

Polo Grounds, New York City, Home of the New York Giants.

THIS VINTAGE POSTCARD SHOWS HOW THE BATHTUB-SHAPED POLO GROUNDS WERE TUCKED INTO A HILLSIDE KNOWN AS COOGAN'S HOLLOW.

"Another thing you can learn from are the messages on the backs of the older postcards," Crabtree said. "I have many in my collection that talk about various players or historical events—Joe DiMaggio's hitting streak, Mickey Mantle hitting one out of Tiger Stadium, World Series wins. These say a lot, in turn, about American society at the time."

Sitting on History

Paul Ferrante, a Connecticut middle school teacher, has collected actual seats from fifteen different ballparks. His collection includes other stadium artifacts, too.

"My favorite, most unique item? That'd be an actual turnstile from Philadelphia's Shibe Park, used in 1909," Ferrante said. "That was a challenge, getting that down into my basement!"

Of all stadium seats, Ferrante has found three that draw extra collector interest. End-aisle seats in the Polo Grounds featured a cast-iron "NY" under the armrest. Aisle seats in Crosley Field displayed a "C" with "Reds" showing in the middle of the letter. And in Tiger Stadium, a batting tiger was shown on each side of the seat, in three-dimensional fashion.

Ferrante has collected the history of ballparks, too. He has a copy of an early 1970s advertisement from Winston cigarettes. The ad instructs fans to bring five empty cigarette carton boxes, $7.50, and tax to a Korvette's department store in the New York area to get an actual seat from Yankee Stadium. At the time, new seats were being installed during a two-year makeover of the stadium.

How can a fan find seats from long-gone team homes? Ferrante reads old newspapers, studying the demolition dates of ballparks that teams have abandoned. He has learned that seats have been reused in minor league stadiums, schools, parks—even a prison. Perhaps, one day, these places will discard the seats, too.

Old seats. Old postcards. As more ballparks disappear, you can be sure that fans and collectors will find more ways to keep their memories alive.

7

BALLPARK BILLS

Whose stadium is it? The home team's, right?

This is baseball's classic trick question. While it's easy to know which teams *use* a stadium, it's harder to know who paid to *build* the stadium, or who actually *controls* the place.

Citizens Pay

These days, stadiums are given—or rented—to teams. Either option allows teams to leave at almost any time.

Fearing that their team may leave if someone else promises a bigger and better stadium, fans may wonder, Why not give the team what it wants and build a bigger stadium? Even though the costs could be great, the city could get something out of the deal.

What could a city get? For starters, it could get yearly rent. In addition, city leaders often hope out-of-town fans stay and spend before and after games. If tourists are eating, shopping, and sightseeing, this could mean more money for local businesses, more tax revenue for the city, and maybe more jobs, too.

If the new ballpark seats a few extra thousand fans, wouldn't fans benefit, too? Wouldn't there be more tickets to go around?

Perhaps. But how much would those new tickets cost? Sections offering the lowest-price bleacher seats often shrink in new stadium designs. Added seats may be for luxury boxes (suites) or season tickets. And even fans who can afford those seats behind the dugout may not have a chance to

MIDWAY THROUGH THE 1999 SEASON, THE MARINERS MOVED INTO SAFECO FIELD. THE NEW FACILITY, WHICH HOLDS OVER 45,000 IN GRANDSTAND SEATING, FEATURES A RETRACTABLE ROOF, GIVING THE M'S THE CHOICE OF INDOOR OR OUTDOOR PLAY.

buy them for twenty to twenty-five years. That's how long a personal seat license (PSL) usually lasts.

A PSL gives a fan the right to purchase a certain seat for a set number of years. That person will always have first chance to buy that seat. That right costs thousands of dollars. The tickets for games cost more on top of that.

The PSL often benefits businesses. A business can afford to buy both the PSL and the tickets, and can use those tickets to entertain customers or to give away as prizes.

And the team's business benefits by having the money from the PSL.

Not So Fast

Sometimes new stadiums have undesired effects. They can cost more than expected, eat up taxpayer money intended for other purposes, and lead to budget battles.

The war over paying for new stadiums may continue even after the first game is played on the new field. Such battles went on in Seattle when the Mariners' Safeco Field, born in 1999, was less than a year old.

The ballpark, complete with a retractable roof, cost $517 million, some $100 million over the original estimate. "Cost overruns" is the construction term for extra costs. The Mariners said the city or state government should pay all of the overruns, too. The state of

DO YOU OWN A TEAM, AND WANT YOUR CITY AND STATE TO PAY FOR YOUR BALLPARK?

HERE ARE SOME IDEAS TEAMS HAVE SUGGESTED:

TOURIST TAX: FOR HOTELS OR RENTAL CARS.

SALES TAX: CITIZENS ARE TAXED ON ALL THEY BUY.

TICKET TAX: FANS WHO COME TO YOUR BALLPARK WILL PAY EVEN MORE.

LOTTERY TICKETS: THIS WAS BALTIMORE'S GAMBLE.

SIN TAX: A FIFTEEN-YEAR TAX ON CIGARETTES AND ALCOHOL IN THE SURROUNDING COUNTY WAS SET TO RAISE $84 MILLION TO BUILD CLEVELAND'S JACOBS FIELD.

TIF: TAX INCREMENTAL FINANCING USES TAXES ALREADY COLLECTED FOR NEW CONSTRUCTION. OF COURSE, THE MONEY HAS TO BE TAKEN FROM OTHER PUBLIC-FUNDED SERVICES, LIKE SCHOOLS.

Washington said the Mariners were responsible.

More stadium financing disputes started brewing as the 2000 season began. In Florida, the Marlins drew 35,000 fans to their home opener. But the same day, Governor Jeb Bush wrote a column for the team's hometown newspaper, the *Miami Herald*. Bush stated that he'd be against any tax used to raise money for a new ballpark.

Fans took the message as a good-bye to the Marlins. If the state wouldn't help build a ballpark, the team might move to a city and state that offered newer, better facilities. Attendance dropped quickly over the next three games. Why support a team that was probably leaving?

The year before, Marlins owner John Henry had already put whole new twists on ballpark-financing traditions when he told reporters that he'd return 90 percent of team profits to the public—if the public helped pay for the team's new ballpark.

"I've always said I'm not in it for the money," the owner claimed. "My philosophy is that the team is a public asset. It belongs to the community." The owner even added that, if his stadium offer were accepted, the city would get its share of the profit if he sold the team! However, the Marlins owner noted that he expected to lose between $5 million and $9 million in the 2000 season. Would the public be earning 90 percent of nothing, if the Marlins kept losing money each year?

But, either way, the public wasn't having a lot of say. Money talks. And money can decide who else gets to talk. The decision about which taxes would help finance the public portion of the Marlins' hoped-for stadium was a battle among businessmen. When the team suggested increasing the tax on car rentals by $1, former Marlins owner Wayne Huizenga, who owned two national car rental companies, opposed the tax increase.

Huizenga didn't want the Marlins to have a new stadium anyway. For Huizenga also owned Pro Player stadium, the place the Marlins wanted to leave. Huizenga didn't want to lose rent from eighty-one Marlins home games per year.

In the Midwest, the Cardinals tried a somewhat unusual game plan. After winning four of their first five games in 2000, the team unveiled plans for a new stadium. The Cards vowed they would not ask St. Louis to levy new taxes. But, quietly, the team hoped that the city would make $5 to $6 million available from the general fund—of tax dollars—to care for the stadium.

THE TIGERS FIRST GAME IN THEIR NEW BALLPARK WAS A WIN AGAINST THE MARINERS IN APRIL 2000. COMERICA FEATURES A "FREE SAMPLE" DESIGN, MADE SO PEOPLE WITHOUT TICKETS CAN GET A PEEK OF THE ACTION FROM OUTSIDE THE PARK.

THE MINNESOTA TWINS WANTED A NEW OUTDOOR STADIUM. VOTERS WERE ASKED TO APPROVE A SALES TAX INCREASE TO HELP PAY FOR THE BALLPARK. TO ENCOURAGE THE IDEA, FORMER TWINS APPEARED AT SOFT-BALL GAMES, WHERE CITIZENS COULD GET FREE AUTOGRAPHS AND FREE HOT DOGS. STILL, THE ISSUE FAILED, GETTING ONLY 42 PERCENT APPROVAL.

Battle Over Fenway

"Save Fenway Park" is the name of a volunteer citizen group opposing the destruction of the famed Boston ballpark. The group began the 2000 baseball season with its own educational Web site, www.savefenwaypark.com. The citizens knew the Red Sox wanted a stadium like other newer stadiums they'd seen—locales with moneymaking abilities such as more concessions and restaurants. The team voiced plans to have such a place to begin the 2003 season. The "Save Fenway Park" group chose to present a plan of its own—making the public aware of how a new stadium would be built. What would the ballpark cost the team, and citizens?

"The cost of the stadium itself is placed at $353 million. This is what the Sox plan to take on as their share, and nothing else. They will finance this with bank loans, naming rights, and personal seat licenses," group spokesman Dan Wilson said.

The team will pay for the stadium. What's wrong with that? Wilson went on to note that the team asked the state to pay $82 million for parking structures and another $53 million for roads, traffic lights, and other changes needed in the area to service a new ballpark. And the Red Sox wanted Boston to pay for the purchase and clearing of the space needed—no matter what the cost. This could reach $150 million—or more.

The "Save Fenway Park" group objected to this idea. What money would be left for schools if the city has huge building debts to pay?

The Red Sox dropped the name "Fenway Park" when discussing the new ballpark idea. The team admitted it would consider selling naming rights to help pay bills.

Teams often count "naming rights" as part of their possible funding money. Teams can sell their ballpark's name to the highest bidder. Comerica Financial

Services paid $66 million to name Comerica Park for thirty years, which means that, for thirty years, Comerica's name would be printed and spoken every time a game was reported on radio, TV, or in print.

The $23 million Dodger Stadium, built in Los Angeles in 1962 by the team-owning O'Malley family, was the last baseball facility constructed without taxes. As cities rush to please their teams, fearing that the lack of a ballpark could cause the team to move, Dodger Stadium may hold that record for years to come.

THE AVERAGE TICKET PRICE FOR A MAJOR LEAGUE GAME ROSE BY 11.8 PERCENT FOR THE 2000 SEASON. THE RED SOX TOPPED THE CHARTS WITH AN AVERAGE TICKET PRICE OF $28.33. NEW STADIUMS TOOK THEIR TOLL ON FANS, THOUGH. COMPARE AVERAGE TICKET PRICES FROM 1999 WITH THOSE OF OLD PARKS:

TICKETS FOR TIGERS GAMES AT COMERICA PARK ROSE FROM AN AVERAGE $12.23 TO $24.83—UP 103 PERCENT.

TICKETS TO THE PACIFIC BELL PARK IN SAN FRANCISCO AVERAGED $21.24, UP FROM $12.12 A YEAR EARLIER, A 75 PERCENT INCREASE.

IN HOUSTON, ENRON FIELD TICKETS AVERAGED $20.01, UP FROM THE $13.30 AVERAGE IN THE ASTRODOME, A 50 PERCENT INCREASE.

8

IMAGINING BALLPARKS

Watch the other diners next time you eat out. The people at the next table just might be planning a ballpark.

Frank Scicchitano was a project designer for Atlanta's Turner Field, the Braves home since April 4, 1997. "I was one of four full-time people [from Ellerbe Becket—an architectural company]," he said. He remembers his co-workers as a "passionate" group.

"We would work until 9 or 10 P.M. many nights," he said. "We ate at every restaurant in Atlanta. We liked restaurants with paper tablecloths so we could draw on them. Even after work, we still discussed the ballpark's design." The designers would take their tablecloth creations home, then back to work the next day.

Scicchitano spent a year in Atlanta. "We say that 50 percent of designing is done in the field [at the site]," he said. During his stay, he saw a couple of games at Fulton County Stadium, the Braves ballpark that was going to be replaced. The stadium had been used by the Braves since 1966.

"That was designed and built in just twenty-two months!" Scicchitano said. "It was nice for its era." But Scicchitano described it as a "one-size-fits-all" type of stadium.

Such stadiums were civic buildings built by municipalities (city government), he explained. "Designers 'dumbed' the buildings down, to suit as many tenants as possible. The stadiums couldn't be all things to all people." The result? Seats in some

THE BRICK-AND-LIMESTONE EXTERIOR OF ATLANTA'S THREE-LEVEL BALLPARK HAS A RETRO LOOK. INSIDE, THE BRAVE'S COLORS ARE REFLECTED IN THE SEATS (DARK BLUE WITH RED NUMBERS), LOTS OF UNPAINTED CONCRETE, AND A WHITE TRACK.

stadiums had bad sightlines. Even worse, the stadiums had no "personality." Even the home teams felt like visitors. Why clutter the place up with baseball decor if the circus was going to move in next week?

Double Duty

The Ellerbe Becket firm joined with three other architectural groups to design the new Turner Field, which, at first, would be used for different events during the 1996 Olympics. Then a partial tear-down and conversion would create a ballpark for the Braves alone, just eight months later. The recycling plan kept costs to $235 million.

Scicchitano's design specialty was the concourse, the hallwaylike spaces that get fans from the gates to their seats. "We wanted people to stop and gather. We wanted to make the wait more pleasant. We wanted people to have a reason to leave their seats. Baseball is the only game with rain delays. We wanted fans to stick around." Scicchitano added, "Today's buildings are entertainment buildings." In other words, concourses should be filled with other things for fans to do who can't or don't want to watch the game. Shopping, eating, interactive games, exhibits— Turner Field would have the appeal of a mall.

Although Ellerbe Becket had never designed a major league ballpark before, Scicchitano had experienced some of baseball's most famous facilities. "When I was growing up, my dad took me to Yankee Stadium, Shea Stadium, and the Polo Grounds," he said.

His father had visited Ebbets Field, and told him about the torn-down ballpark. Today, Scicchitano said, many teams ask for stadiums designed "like Ebbets."

"Lots of people romanticize Ebbets Field," said Scicchitano, noting that the design of the Mets' proposed new stadium and the Brewers' new Miller Park are both based on Ebbets Field.

Although the limestone and brick exterior of Turner Field is compared more to Baltimore's Camden Yards or Colorado's Coors Field, the Atlanta creators inserted old-fashioned echoes of Ebbets in the interior. Some steel beams are green, as is the roof canopy, saluting the natural grass field. But all seats are dark blue with red numeral markings. Much of the concrete is unpainted. The result is a basic red, white, and blue theme, stressing the team colors.

But does "retro" talk of making new ballparks like old extend past looks?

"When someone says 'retro,' people are wanting brick, archways, and steel beams," Scicchitano said. "I think of 'retro' as a ballpark built with the materials of that time period, built with the *community* in mind, designed around the game. They were more community-friendly. To me, [Cleveland's] Jacobs Field is a retro building. The Atlanta ballpark's retro touch, linking it to the city's past, can be found in the park's dozen monuments saluting Olympic moments. The ballpark itself is a monument to those games. "We were driven by the legacy of the Olympics," Scicchitano said. "It was our goal to reuse as much as we humanly could."

A Ballpark Named B.O.B.

Less than one year later, on March 31, 1998, another Ellerbe Becket creation joined baseball's ballpark family. A husband and wife team—Diane and Michael Jacobs—were part of the creative process for Bank One Ballpark (also known as B.O.B.) in Phoenix.

Diane Jacobs said, "The design process began as a competition, which was won by Ellerbe Becket. Part of the contract involved moving a [design] team to the city. We [in the design team] shared office space with the Diamondbacks. I arrived in May 1995 in Arizona."

At the time, Michael Jacobs said, he was "helping design the Milwaukee Brewers spring training complex. I came on to the Diamondbacks project in February, 1996." By the end of the design phase, close to thirty people were involved.

The architects divided the workload by dividing the future park into levels and sectors. Those assignments reveal which person designed which part of the park. Michael helped design the museum and interactive entertainment areas of the ballpark. Diane's responsibilities included suite design.

One design challenge was to include an old building nearby, the Arizona Citrus Growers Building. Opponents of using public funds to help build the ballpark thought that getting the Citrus building on the National Historic Register would stop the team from building.

But acquiring the Citrus building for use as part of the ballpark was a winning response. The design team decided it could use the warehouse as a lifeline to the ballpark. It's still a warehouse of sorts, designed as sort of the belly of the ballpark, holding supplies for concession stands. The team's strategy to adopt the building stopped foes of the ballpark.

Both of the Jacobses formerly lived in Boston. Past visits to Fenway Park inspired their work. Michael said, "Living in Boston, we saw games at Fenway Park. The bowl is intimate, and the ballpark is in the fabric

of the city." During their work in Arizona, "We toured Coors, Jacobs Field, and Camden Yards, too." Diane added, "We heard those names from the teams constantly." In other words, the Diamondbacks wouldn't complain if their new facility looked slightly like those successful stadiums.

In the end, Ellerbe Becket created a ballpark quite different from the famed examples. Was the new B.O.B. another huge box, just like all the other buildings in the Phoenix warehouse district? Not necessarily. It was a stadium with looks and personality like few others.

Yes, the measurements of the ballpark are huge—more than 800 by 750 feet (244 by 229 meters) and 270 feet (82 meters) tall. The boxlike shape was anything but another circular 1970s multipurpose stadium design. However, the designers wanted a unique ballpark exterior which could be seen and appreciated by one individual on the ground. Seeking materials common to Arizona, they created the ballpark's exterior with a blend of stone, glass, brick, and metal wall. On B.O.B.'s north side, facing downtown, 60-by-60-foot (18-by-18-meter) murals were added. Walking past, an individual could view smaller, distinct portions of the structure—not always possible with skyscrapers.

Inside the structure, 85 percent of the ballpark's 48,569 seats were located between the foul poles—putting more fans in the action. Fan comfort for both genders was central in the design. While 55 toilets and 221 urinals were created for men, a total of 340 women's toilets were included. Fans would no longer miss much of the game stuck in a restroom line.

A Roof and A Pool

Although the Jacobses helped with the ballpark design, both architects sounded like any devoted fan when discussing the ballpark's two most famous features—the gleaming white retractable roof and the pool.

Why a pool? Diane laughed when she first heard that the Diamondbacks wanted a pool in the park. "We thought the team official was joking," she said. But "it was a team sponsor's [advertiser's] idea." Now, she says, "It's the signature look of the ballpark. But you don't see a lot of people swimming." Michael guessed that when the roof closes and the air conditioning comes on, it might be too cool to swim. Of course, only fans who rent a suite with the pool are allowed to swim.

RETRACTABLE ROOFS CAN PREVENT MANY PROBLEMS. THE TORONTO BLUE JAYS OPENED THE SKYDOME ROOF FOR A NIGHT GAME ON AUGUST 27, 1990. CLOUDS OF GNATS STOPPED THE GAME IN THE FIFTH INNING. CLOSING THE ROOF STOPPED THE BUGS AND ALLOWED THE GAME TO RESUME.

Why a retractable roof? "To grow natural grass," Michael explained. On hot days, the roof provides shade for the fans. But at other times it can be opened to let the sun shine on the natural grass field.

"What's beautiful is that opening or closing the roof uses only about $2 worth of electricity. It's simple shipyard technology, like a pulley system. The telescoping roof panels are lighter, faster, and cheaper" than newer mechanical methods of creating retractable roofs.

When the roof is opened to the sky or closed "the crowd atmosphere changes," explained Diane. First, "there is silence." But then dramatic music and thunderous creaking effects are played over the loudspeakers. "It really bummed the design team the first time they heard this!" added Diane, because the roof is actually "quiet in motion."

She sees only one small fault in B.O.B.'s top. "The roof is white. That might have been a mistake," Diane said. "Like white baseball uniforms, the roof doesn't stay that color for long."

The Jacobses remained Arizona residents after the ballpark was designed. "We walked the site. It's gratifying now to see people in those seats," Diane said.

Michael laughed. "But after giving up four and a half years of your life, it gets personal. You want to say, 'This is mine. Wait a minute!' They are in your home."

Diane agreed. "Now, we have to have a ticket, or wear a pass to be there."

Three members of the Jacobs family saw the Diamondbacks open Bank One Ballpark. "Our son was three months old on opening day," Diane said. "We put him in a pouch to carry him to the ballpark. Some people thought we were crazy, but we wanted him to be there, too. It was his ballpark, too. He calls it 'My Baseball Building.'"

9

STADIUM 2000: THE FIRST THREE

The year 2000. One new season. Three new ballparks. Not since 1977, when baseball welcomed two new expansion teams, did fans see so many changes of address. In that year the Seattle Mariners debuted in the Kingdome, the Toronto Blue Jays opened in eighteen-year-old Exhibition Stadium, and the Montreal Expos moved into Olympic Stadium.

Pacific Bell Park
San Francisco, California
Would the Giants' new park be just as windy as their old home, Candlestick Park?

The team had lived with the park known as "The Stick" from 1960 to 1999. Its building site on Candlestick Point had been approved by team vice president Chub Feeney after a visit on an unusually calm morning. He was unaware of the winds that blow off the Pacific Ocean in afternoons and evenings. During the 1961 All-Star game, the wind knocked Giants pitcher Stu Miller off the mound!

Bruce White, a University of California professor of mechanical and aeronautical engineering, made sure players could stay upright in the new stadium. White studied a 4-inch (7.6-centimeter) model of the nearby neighborhood. He realized that, as conceived, the proposed park was likely to face winds twice as fierce as Candlestick's. The solution: Turn the stadium to face east, eliminating exposure to the worst northwesterly winds.

THE SAN FRANCISCO RECREATION AND PARKS COMMISSION HELD A CONTEST TO NAME THE NEW BALLPARK THE GIANTS WOULD OPEN IN 1960. THEY GOT MORE THAN 20,000 ENTRIES AND 2,000 NAMES. THE WINNER: CANDLESTICK PARK, AFTER THE BALLPARK'S LOCATION, CANDLESTICK POINT.

FORGET SAN FRANCISCO'S McCOVEY'S COVE. MONTREAL'S JARRY PARK OFFERED THE FIRST WATER TARGET FOR HOME RUN ARTISTS FROM 1969 TO 1976. BEYOND THE RIGHT FIELD FENCE OF THE FORMER CITY BALLPARK WAS A PUBLIC SWIMMING POOL.

The new ballpark kept its connection with the Pacific Ocean, though. Home run balls that cleared the 307-foot (94-meter) right field fence could land right in the bay. Actually, the ocean inlet is the China Basin Channel. The team dubbed the target "McCovey's Cove," after ex-Giants slugger and Hall of Famer Willie McCovey.

But San Francisco players soon wondered if they might pay the price for having the

fans too close to the action in the new ballpark. Giants left fielder Barry Bonds was robbed during an April home game—by a Giants fan. A 335-foot (102-meter) line drive was too tempting for a teenager who leaned over the 8-foot (2.4-meter) left field fence and snatched it right in front of Bonds. The result? A three-run homer giving the Diamondbacks a 7–4 win over the hosting Giants.

Enron Field
Houston, Texas
To honor Houston's railroad history and the nearby Union Station, Enron Field features a replica of an 1800s locomotive that chugs beyond the left field wall. Running on 800 feet (244 meters) of track, the steam engine celebrates Astro homers. And, when the retractable roof begins to close, the train puffs across the track as if it's pulling the roof.

But it was Houston's field design that ignited baseball imaginations. In tribute to the looks of the famous old Cincinnati Reds' ballpark, Crosley Field, Enron has a small hill near the center field fence—a 30-degree slope on a 10-foot incline.

Gone from this park was the artificial turf that bore the Astros' name. Players liked the natural grass. And hitters drooled over the left field fence just 315 feet (96 meters) away—the shortest in the National League. A 21-foot-high (6-meter) scoreboard offered a slight obstacle, but prospective sluggers kept dreaming.

The first homestand in April showed Enron's promise for power hits. A three-game matchup against the Cardinals sparked eighteen homers. In thirty-five seasons in the Astrodome, teams had never produced more than a dozen homers in a three-game set.

Comerica Park
Detroit, Michigan
The Tigers didn't forget the past with their new ballpark. Stainless-steel statues of team legends including

Al Kaline, Hal Newhouser, Hank Greenberg, and Ty Cobb stand outside the center field wall.

So what was new? A Ferris wheel and other amusement-parklike additions, even a carousel with thirty tigers! The scoreboard was to be the largest of any in baseball, with two 5,000-pound tiger statues perched atop, flashing fierce electric eyes.

The ballpark seats just 40,000, with no upper deck like Tiger Stadium used to have. However, open spaces in the new park allow fans on the outside to get free peeks at the action on the field. Unlike San Francisco and Houston, Detroit did not get a homer-friendly park. Tigers outfielder Bobby Higginson joked about the size of the new park, calling it "Comerica National Park."

A fourth ballpark failed in its bid to join the 2000 newcomers. Milwaukee's Miller Park had been progressing on schedule in its 1999 construction. Then, on July 14, 1999, Wisconsin winds reaching 26 miles per hour toppled a giant crane that was placing part of the upper deck roof on the new park. Two workers died, and some $100 million in damages resulted in months of delays. Fans who had said good-bye to County Stadium found themselves saying hello to one more season in the team's only home since 1970.

Milwaukee would open a new park in 2001. So would Pittsburgh. Meanwhile, other teams studied how the Giants afforded a ballpark with only $10 million in tax money. The Tigers gave tours to other team owners and reporters, to marvel at the Comerica design.

In a new century, a new ballpark seemed like a sure way to compete for wins—and profits.

IS BASEBALL FULL OF UPS AND DOWNS? IT IS AT DETROIT'S COMERICA PARK, WHICH FEATURES A FERRIS WHEEL AND CAROUSEL.

10

TOMORROW'S BALLPARKS

What does the twenty-first century hold for ballparks? Recent baseball stadium history offers a few hints:

Theme Park Stars

In 1998, the Atlanta Braves joined Mickey Mouse's team. The Braves adopted Walt Disney World's "Wide World of Sports Complex" as a spring training home. The Braves sold tickets to batting practice—a free treat at most preseason locations.

The theme park idea wasn't new. In the 1980s, an amusement park in Florida served as the Kansas City Royals' spring training headquarters. But, in 1988, the Royals moved to Baseball City, a facility built to their exact wishes. Without a team to attract tourists, "Boardwalk and Baseball," as the old complex was called, went out of business.

The Tigers stadium that opened in 2000 offered fans some new amusements—a Ferris wheel and carousel. Don't be surprised if a future ticket bought for a regular-season game at a ballpark also entitles you to amusement park entertainment!

Innkeepers

Imagine getting out of bed, getting dressed, and walking down the hall to watch a game in a real baseball stadium. Toronto's Skydome pioneered such a concept in 1989. A luxury hotel was built within the stadium.

MAKING BASEBALL ENTERTAINING IS NOTHING NEW. BEFORE THE ATHLETICS MOVED TO OAKLAND TO BEGIN 1968, THIS FELLOW TURNED KANSAS CITY'S MUNICIPAL STADIUM INTO AN AMUSEMENT PARK OF SORTS. WHO WAS HE? A MECHANICAL RABBIT, WHO WOULD POP UP FROM BEHIND HOME PLATE, SERVING FRESH BASEBALLS TO THE UMPIRE!

LOOK FOR MORE FUTURE BALL-PARKS TO HAVE BASEBALL-RELATED STREET NAMES. BOSTON'S FENWAY PARK IS AT 4 YAWKEY WAY, NAMED FOR FORMER OWNER TOM YAWKEY.

Of the hotel's 348 rooms, 70 had views of the field. It was possible to wake up and see the Blue Jays play by looking out the window of your own room. Fans in regular seats have had occasional shocks. Looking out past the center field wall at the expensive rooms, they've noticed lodgers lacking clothes. But Skydome rooms do have curtains!

Shopping Malls

Once ballparks offered mostly baseball. Hot dog and popcorn stands and vendors used to be easier to find outside stadiums than in the ballpark aisles. Souvenirs, such as caps and T-shirts, were even tougher to get in ballparks.

By the 1960s things began to change. Concession stands moved indoors. Now when new ballparks are built, retail space is allowed for restaurants and shops. Although shops have remained baseball-related, teams may broaden their sales pitches in the future. If a family goes to the game, and some family members don't want to see baseball, no problem. They could visit a different store every inning.

Tropicana Field, home of the Tampa Bay Devil Rays, showed the possibilities for such a concept in 1999. After eight years of being an ordinary domed stadium, the Florida facility added a stadium restaurant overlooking center field, a cigar bar, a barber shop, a brew pub, a sports bar, a video arcade, a post office, and a bank branch—all within the complex.

Museums

Famed players and winning teams from the past might be more than history in future ballparks. Past heroes may be ticket-selling tools.

Newer stadiums may be too young to have hosted historic events in their short lives. But the teams can reassure fans and honor the past by including a team hall of fame within the ballpark with statues of previous stars, or displays that salute winning teams from years ago. The ballpark that respects history tells a fan that even if the players don't look good just now, they shouldn't give up. There's a tradition of winning here. Who knows when it could happen again?

One of the first ideas batted about by the Red Sox when designing a new ballpark was preserving a part of old Fenway Park. They suggested saving a chunk of the famous Green Monster, the huge wall in left field.

A Short Life

The Seattle Mariners moved into the multipurpose Kingdome in 1977. In mid-1999, the team got its wish—an open-air facility that didn't have to be shared with other sports teams. The team relocated to the new baseball-only Safeco Field.

The Chicago White Sox opened "new" Comiskey Park in 1991. Before the 1990s were complete, owner Jerry Reinsdorf worried to newspaper reporters that the size of the ballpark limited the team's ticket-selling power.

The moral of the story? Although stadiums may be built to survive decades of use, team owners aren't that patient. Teams expect ballparks to make them money. If the profit dips, the ballpark's life could be a short one.

AFTER SERVING THE MARINERS FOR JUST OVER 20 YEARS, THE SEATTLE KINGDOME WAS DEMOLISHED IN 2000 AND REPLACED BY SAFECO FIELD.

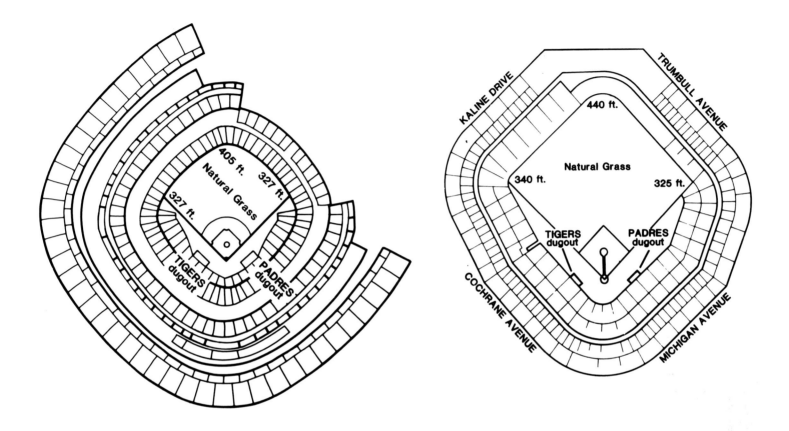

TWO BALLPARKS COMPARED

BASEBALL PARKS CAN BE AS DIFFERENT AS NIGHT AND DAY, EVEN IN DIMENSIONS—AS THIS COMPARISON OF SAN DIEGO'S JACK MURPHY STADIUM (LEFT) AND DETROIT'S TIGER STADIUM (RIGHT) SHOW. WHILE DISTANCES BETWEEN HOME PLATE, THE PITCHER'S MOUND, AND THE BASES MUST BE THE SAME IN ALL PARKS, ONLY CERTAIN MINIMUM DISTANCES MUST BE MAINTAINED FROM HOME PLATE TO THE NEAREST FENCE, STAND, OR OTHER OBSTRUCTION ON THE FOUL LINES (325 FEET, OR 99 METERS) AND TO THE CENTER FIELD FENCE (400 FEET, OR 122 METERS).

For Further Information

Books

Cagan, Joanna and Neil deMause. *Field of Schemes: How the Great Stadium Swindle Turns Public Money into Private Profit.* Monroe, ME: Common Courage Press, 1998.

Lowry, Philip J. *Green Cathedrals.* Reading, MA: Addison Wesley, 1992.

Nowlin, Bill, Mike Ross, and Jim Prime. *Fenway Saved.* Champaign, IL: Sports Publishing Inc., 1999.

Reidenbaugh, Lowell. *Take Me Out to the Ball Park.* St. Louis, MO: The Sporting News, 1983.

Ritter, Lawrence S. *Lost Ballparks: A Celebration of Baseball's Legendary Fields.* New York: Viking, Studio Books, 1992.

Weiner, Jay. *Stadium Games: Fifty Years of Big League Greed and Bush League Boondoggles.* Minneapolis: University of Minnesota Press, 2000.

Smith, Ron. *The Ballpark Book: A Journey Through the Fields of Baseball Magic.* St. Louis, The Sporting News, 2000.

The Ballparks Postcards Checklist and Price Guide. For information on the current edition, contact author Tom Crabtree at 1667 NW Iowa Ave., Bend, OR 97701.

Internet

www.ballparks.com
A superstar among Web sites, this address brings you to an amazing collection of photos, newspaper articles, team statistics, and fan observations about past, present, and future baseball stadiums.

www.baseballparks.com
This fun, thoughtful site includes "Changes," where upcoming and rumored ballpark moves are noted. "New Park Ideas" shares the extraordinary ballpark design ideas of ordinary fans.

www.bestweb.net/~dimike/fod/
Take a picture, make a memory. This fan shares his ballpark trips with everyone, photographing each baseball journey and posting the pictures.

www.crosleyfield.com
Although Crosley's last season was 1970, this torn-down classic comes alive again in its cyberspace home. Current photos from the ballpark's location show "then and now" views from what were once various seats throughout Crosley Field.

www.fieldofschemes.com
From the authors of a book by the same name, this Web site exposes teams that convince city and state governments to pay most of the bills when new ballparks are built.

www.hoksport.com
Get current news from the designers of some of baseball's newest stadiums.

www.majorleaguebaseball.com
Teams from the American and National League have individual Web sites. Many of these sites have information about the team's ballpark.

www.mindspring.com/~raisingirl/stadium.htm
Don't let the address fool you. This is where a fan has created a stirring tribute to an underappreciated ballpark. The Web site is titled "Atlanta Fulton County Stadium, 1965-1997."

www.sabr.org
Members of the Society for American Baseball Research (SABR) study many aspects of the sport. The Ballparks Committee, made up of fans of all ages, researches past, present, and future baseball stadiums.

Index